Meet the All-Stars:

The Greatest Basketball Players of Our Time

By A.E. Arost

A Boxscorepress Book

A Boxscorepress Book
365 Richland Ave
San Francisco, California 94110

ISBN: 978-0692669945

Photographs in this collection have appeared in
Wikimedia Commons, Diggita.it, and Flickr.

First Edition 2016.
Designed by Jessica Moreland

Printed in the United States of America
via CreateSpace®, an Amazon company.

FOR HENRY, MY FAVORITE BOO

TABLE OF CONTENTS

The West's Reserves

Injured Players

Extra, Extra!

INTRODUCTION

The All-Stars are the greatest basketball players of our time. Each year, the best players of the Eastern and Western Conferences come together to play an epic exhibition game that drives fans wild! This book focuses on the latest All-Stars: the 2016 players who participated in the 65th NBA All-Star Game.

How are the All-Stars Chosen?

Basketball fans choose the starting players for the East team and the West team by voting for them online via NBA.com or through an approved social media site. The two guards and three frontcourt players (centers and forwards) to receive the most votes in the Eastern and Western Conferences are the starters for each team. That means *you* get to decide who the starters will be in each and every All-Star game!

The head coaches for all the teams in their own Conferences vote on the reserves, or second-string players. They select two additional guards, three frontcourt players, and two wild card players to play in the game.

Are your basketball heroes the dominating ballers who've rocked the basketball world for years: LeBron James, Dwyane Wade, Kobe Bryant, or Chris Paul? Or do you love to watch it rain when #30, the amazing Stephen Curry, breaks the record for the most three-point shots in a year? Or maybe you wear the defensive forward jerseys of Kawhi Leonard or Draymond Green? No matter who your favorites are, you can vote them onto the All-Star team and see them all play in one game! If you didn't vote this year, be sure to vote next year for *your* favorite player. And invite your friends to watch the big game.

The 2016 All-Star Game

The 2016 All-Star Basketball Game was an impressive, record-breaking game. It was hosted outside the United States for the first time ever in Toronto, Canada on February 14, 2016. Combined, the players scored the most points in All-Star game history, with a total of 369 points between the East and West teams. The West beat the East 196-173. On top of the lively, high-scoring game, the weekend was filled with other magical milestones, including Aaron Gordon's performance in the Slam Dunk Contest, which left viewers, commentators, and the All-Stars themselves with their mouths hanging open. Inside this book, you will find the low down on many other memorable moments of this unforgettable All-Star weekend!

Inside this Book

Becoming an All-Star is a special honor. This book highlights all the players in the 2016 All-Star Game. Here you will find information on each player's unique skills.*

**TURN THE PAGE TO MEET THE ALL-STARS,
THE GREATEST BASKETBALL PLAYERS OF OUR TIME!**

* All the players' statistics were accurate as of February 14, 2016.

THE EAST'S STARTERS

LEBRON JAMES | CAVALIERS

Forward	From: St. Vincent-St. Mary High School (Akron, Ohio)	
WT: 250 lbs.	HT: 6 ft. 8 in.	BIRTHDATE: 12/30/84

LeBron Raymone James, better known as "King James," received the most votes of any basketball player in the Eastern conference for the 2016 NBA All-Star Game. He was selected to be an All-Star in his second season in the League in 2004, and he has been an All-Star every year since—that means he's been an All-Star for a total of twelve years in a row! In the 2016 game, James moved ahead to become the all-time leading scorer in the All-Star games, passing Kobe Bryant.

After growing up in Akron, Ohio, his home team, the Cleveland Cavaliers **drafted** him with the 1st overall pick straight out of high school. He was named the NBA **Rookie** of the Year right out of the gate, becoming the youngest player to receive the award. He was also recognized as the Eastern Conference Rookie of the Month for all six months his first season! Four years after joining the team, James led the Cavs to their first-ever NBA Finals, but they lost to the San Antonio Spurs.

WHAT MAKES HIM AN ALL-STAR?

🏀 He holds first place all-time in career assists by a **forward**. He is the only player in NBA history to have over 2000 points, 500 rebounds, 500 assists, and 100 steals in four consecutive seasons.

🏀 He is a four-time winner of the NBA Most Valuable Player (MVP) award.

🏀 James is a big-time **philanthropist**. He started his own foundation to raise money for children's education and has donated millions of dollars to support various charities.

Needing a change of scenery, James took his skills to the Miami Heat, and they reached the NBA Finals all four years he was there. They won the championship two years in a row, in 2012 and 2013. After his last season with the Heat, James decided to go back home to Cleveland in hopes of bringing a championship back to his hometown fans. The team reached the NBA Finals his first year back, in 2015, but they lost to the Golden State Warriors. James did his best to carry his team, averaging 35.8 points, 13.3 rebounds, and 8.8 **assists**, the highest collective averages of any player in NBA Finals history!

DWYANE WADE | HEAT

Guard	From: Marquette University (Milwaukee, Wisconsin)	
WT: 220 lbs.	HT: 6 ft. 4 in.	BIRTHDATE: 1/17/82

Dwyane Wade was drafted as the 5th overall pick by the Miami Heat in the 2003 NBA **Draft**. He is known by fans as D-Wade or Flash. His signature move is making difficult lay-ups, even after hard, midair collisions with larger defenders.

D-Wade grew up in Chicago, and he describes his upbringing as very rough. When he got to high school, he was successful as a football player, but he didn't get much playing time as a basketball player until his **junior** year. Wade was not heavily recruited by colleges because of some academic troubles. The **NCAA** requires student athletes to achieve specific grades and standardized test scores in high school in order to participate in college sports. So, Wade couldn't play his first year of college. But he hired a tutor and worked very hard to overcome those challenges. He played in his second year of college.

WHAT MAKES HIM AN ALL-STAR?

- D-Wade was one of two **guards** to block at least 50 shots in 8 different seasons. (Michael Jordan was the only other guard to achieve this distinction.)

- He raises money for kids in need, earthquake relief, library funds, and countless other causes.

- He won the Sports Illustrated Sportsman of the Year award in 2006.

In 2003, he brought his school, Marquette University, to the **NCAA Final Four**. It was the school's first appearance in the Final Four in almost twenty-five years. As a result of this success, he was the highest drafted Marquette player in school history. After being drafted by the Heat, Wade helped the team qualify for the playoffs his very first year. Despite his great accomplishments his first year, he was overshadowed by another rookie who also started that year: King James. Wade was only the fourth rookie since the introduction of the **shot clock** to lead his team in scoring and assist averages in the postseason.

The Heat have been to the playoffs ten times since Wade joined the team, and they won the championship three times, in 2006, 2012, and 2013! Wade is also a twelve-time consecutive All-Star!

PAUL GEORGE | PACERS

Forward		From: Fresno State (Fresno, California)
WT: 220 lbs.	HT: 6 ft. 9 in.	BIRTHDATE: 5/2/90

While most kids start playing competitive basketball at a very young age, Paul George started out just playing one-on-one against his older sister in the backyard and with neighborhood kids at the park. He did not actually start playing organized basketball until his first year of high school! Once he started playing for his high school team, he quickly developed into an outstanding player and led them to the league championship. He also became the league's MVP.

While he was recruited to several different colleges, he decided to go to a lesser known basketball school, California State University, Fresno (more commonly known as Fresno State), where he was promised more playing time. The decision turned out to be a good one for George. He became a starter and was named one of the most entertaining players in college basketball by Sports Illustrated.

WHAT MAKES HIM AN ALL-STAR?

- With 9 three-pointers in a single game, he broke the Pacers record previously held by Hall of Famer Reggie Miller.

- While at Fresno State, he had the best single-season free-throw percentage in the program's history.

- PG-13 has big-time fans all across the NBA for his colossal windmill-style dunking!

After playing for two years at Fresno State, George was drafted by the Indiana Pacers as the 10th overall pick in the first round in 2010. During his first two seasons, he mostly played the shooting guard position. When he moved to the small forward position in his junior year, his performance increased tremendously, and he was named the NBA Most Improved Player of the Year. In 2014, George changed his jersey number from 24 to 13, and he received the nickname PG-13.

George was an All-Star in 2013 and 2014, but he missed the game in 2015 when a serious fracture in his right leg caused him to miss most of the season. But he was back again in 2016 and almost broke the All-Star game scoring record.

KYLE LOWRY | RAPTORS

Guard	From: Villanova University (Philadelphia, Pennsylvania)	
WT: 205 lbs.	HT: 6 ft. 0 in.	BIRTHDATE: 3/25/86

Kyle Lowry grew up in Philadelphia, and as a result, he loves to play against the Celtics. He attended Villanova University for two years of college before the Memphis Grizzlies drafted him as the 24th pick in the first round of the 2006 NBA Draft. In just his second year with the Grizzlies, he played all 82 games!

While things seemed to be going well in Memphis, when the team drafted Mike Conley, Jr., the team did not have as much of a role for Lowry. In February 2009, he was traded to the Houston Rockets. He found his place there immediately and helped the team reach the playoffs that same year. They lost to the Lakers, who ultimately won the NBA Championship. He continued to have success with the Rockets until a new coach arrived. Lowry did not get along with the new coach, and he was traded to the Raptors in July 2012.

WHAT MAKES HIM AN ALL-STAR?

- Lowry is Toronto's all-time leader in made three-point **field goals** and **triple-doubles** in a season.

- In the 2015-2016 season, he had at least 1 steal in 24 consecutive games, the longest streak by a Raptor since 2001. (Who set the record for the most consecutive steals in NBA history? Chris Paul with 108 straight games!)

- He received the George Gross Sportsman of the Year award in 2014.

When Lowry got to Toronto, he had a mentor who encouraged him to become a leader. He and DeMar DeRozan (also an All-Star in 2016) got together and decided they would do just that. Together, they helped lead the team to win the Atlantic Division title for the first time in seven years in 2014, and they won again in 2015. Both years, they lost in the first round of the playoffs, but the **backcourt** duo continued to push the team to greater heights. Lowry was rewarded for his efforts with All-Star elections in 2015 and 2016.

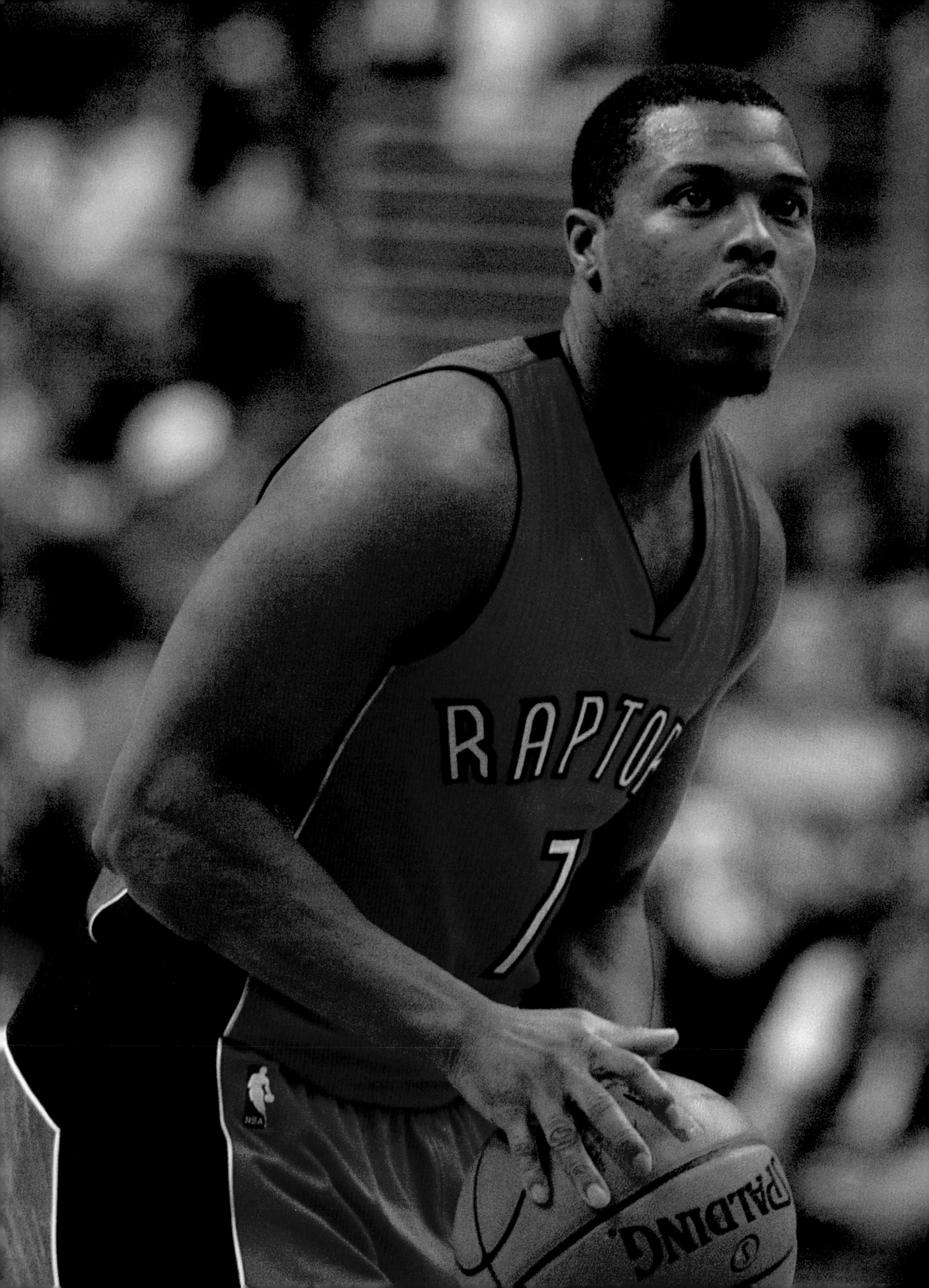

THE EAST'S STARTERS

CARMELO ANTHONY | KNICKS

Forward	From: Syracuse University (Syracuse, New York)	
WT: 240 lbs.	HT: 6 ft. 8 in.	BIRTHDATE: 5/29/84

Carmelo "Melo" Anthony went to Syracuse University. In his **freshman** year, he led the school to its first ever NCAA championship! He was named the most outstanding player of the tournament and was also unanimously voted the NCAA Freshman of the Year.

The next year, in 2003, he was selected as the 3rd pick overall in the NBA Draft by the Denver Nuggets. (The first pick that year was LeBron James). Melo led the Nuggets to the playoffs every year from 2004 to 2010. While with the Nuggets, he became the second youngest player to reach 5,000 points.

In February 2011, Melo was traded to the New York Knicks. It took a couple of years for the Knicks to get back to the playoffs, but in 2013, a year when Melo led the league in scoring, the Knicks made the playoffs again. They lost in the second round.

WHAT MAKES HIM AN ALL-STAR?

- Melo has a charity set up to help disadvantaged children and families. He has also given money to other organizations, including $3 million to his former college!

- He is the only player in NBA history to score over 50 points with no points in the paint, and he is the only player in NBA history to record over 62 points with 0 turnovers in a game.

- He is #30 on the list of all-time NBA leading scorers.

In 2014, Melo became the fiftieth NBA player to score 19,000 career points, and the fifth youngest to achieve the feat. The only younger players to do so were LeBron James, Kobe Bryant, Michael Jordan, and Wilt Chamberlain. Later that year, in 2014, Melo became the fortieth member of the 20,000-point club and the sixth youngest to do so.

Melo has been in nine All-Star games (2007, 2008, 2010-2016).

THE EAST'S RESERVES

DEMAR DEROZAN	Guard	University of Southern California (Los Angeles, CA)	
RAPTORS	WT: 220 lbs.	HT: 6 ft. 7 in.	BIRTHDATE: 8/7/89

🏀 DeMar DeRozan first dunked a basketball in sixth grade!

🏀 At University of Southern California (USC), his 485 points for the season ranked him third and his 201 rebounds ranked him fourth all-time for a USC freshman. Immediately after his freshman year, he decided he would go straight into the NBA, and the Raptors picked him up right away. In his second year, he was the only Raptor to start and play in all 82 games!

🏀 An All-Star in 2014 and 2016, he is best known for his on-the-court partnership with Kyle Lowry; the two players have become a backcourt-scoring machine for the Raptors.

ANDRE DRUMMOND	Center	University of Connecticut (Mansfield, Connecticut)	
PISTONS	WT: 279 lbs.	HT: 6 ft. 11 in.	BIRTHDATE: 8/10/93

🏀 Andre Drummond was born to Jamaican parents. He loves math and computers, and he grew up playing football, soccer, baseball, and lacrosse in addition to basketball!

🏀 He was the first rookie in NBA history to record 18 points and 18 rebounds off the bench. He also had four 20 point-20 rebound games over a two-year period, the most by any player in the NBA during that period of time.

🏀 This year, 2016, is Drummond's first selection to the All-Star game, although he was the MVP of the Rising Star's Challenge game in 2014, with a record 25 rebounds.

PAU GASOL	Center/Forward		Alvirne (Barcelona, Spain)	
BULLS	WT: 250 lbs.	HT: 7 ft. 0 in.	BIRTHDATE: 7/6/80	

🏀 Pau Gasol was born in Spain. He played for his high school team, Alvirne, and then went straight to the Spanish ACB League, which is recognized as the best league in Spain. Gasol was selected 3rd overall in the 2011 NBA Draft and has played for the Memphis Grizzlies and the Los Angeles Lakers. He is currently with the Chicago Bulls.

🏀 Gasol won Rookie of the Year his first season with the Grizzlies. His second year, he scored more points than any other player on the team. During his seven years with the Lakers, he won two NBA Championships.

🏀 Gasol is #54 in career points, #26 in blocks, and #33 in rebounds on the all-time NBA career list! Gasol has been in six All-Star games (2006, 2009-2011, and 2015-2016). In the off-season, he plays for the National Team to keep his skills honed for the NBA season.

AL HORFORD	Center/Forward		University of Florida (Gainesville, Florida)	
HAWKS	WT: 245 lbs.	HT: 6 ft. 10 in.	BIRTHDATE: 6/3/86	

🏀 Al Horford was born to an NBA father: Tito Horford, who played in the NBA for three years. Horford was born in the Dominican Republic and then moved to Michigan when he was fourteen years old; he speaks fluent Spanish and English. He was highly recruited from high school after setting records on his high school team.

🏀 Horford went to University of Florida with basketball players Joakim Noah, Corey Brewer, and David Lee. In his second year, they won the NCAA Championship, and the following year, they became the first college team ever to repeat as national champions with the same starting lineup.

🏀 The Atlanta Hawks drafted Horford 3rd overall in 2007, and he has been playing for them ever since. He is a four-time All-Star (2010-2011 and 2015-2016).

THE EAST'S RESERVES

PAUL MILLSAP	Forward	Louisiana Tech University (Ruston, Louisiana)		
HAWKS	WT: 246 lbs.	HT: 6 ft. 8 in.	BIRTHDATE: 2/10/85	

🏀 Paul Millsap is the only player in NCAA history to lead the nation in rebounding for three straight years!

🏀 The Utah Jazz drafted him after his third year of college; he was the 47th overall pick. He played in Utah for seven years before moving on to the Atlanta Hawks.

🏀 In 2015, Millsap was voted on the All-Star team as a reserve. Three other Atlanta Hawks players were also voted onto the All-Star team that year because the Hawks had a reputation for playing such good "team" basketball. Millsap was also voted on in 2014 and 2016.

ISAIAH THOMAS	Guard	University of Washington (Seattle, Washington)		
CELTICS	WT: 185 lbs.	HT: 5 ft. 9 in.	BIRTHDATE: 2/7/89	

🏀 Isaiah Thomas, who was picked last in the 2011 NBA Draft, won the NBA Rookie of the Month award in February and March 2012. It was the first time a player chosen last in the draft ever won the award, let alone two months in a row!

🏀 Two years later, in March 2014, Thomas became the shortest player ever to achieve a triple-double in the NBA. That same year, Thomas joined a small club of only four other players under 6 ft. 0 in. to average at least 20 points and 6 assists per game in a season.

🏀 Thomas played for the Sacramento Kings for three years before he was traded to the Phoenix Suns and then again to the Boston Celtics. He was named an All-Star in 2016 for his outstanding contributions.

JOHN WALL	Guard	University of Kentucky (Lexington, Kentucky)
WIZARDS	WT: 195 lbs.	HT: 6 ft. 4 in.	BIRTHDATE: 9/6/90

John Wall had a tough childhood, which led him to have some trouble in school. He was cut from his high school basketball team for behavior and attitude problems. He transferred schools and found a good coach who helped him move past those challenges.

He was the 1st overall pick in 2010, selected by the Washington Wizards. In his first three games, he became the second player in NBA history to get 9 assists in each game. In the third game of the season, Wall tied a **franchise** record with 9 steals in a single game. Later that same year, he became the third youngest player to score a triple-double in NBA history. He was off to a tremendous start!

Wall was selected for the All-Star team three years in a row (2014-2016). In 2014, he won the NBA Slam Dunk Contest with a double pump reverse and the help of the Wizards' mascot.

KOBE BRYANT | LAKERS

Forward/Guard	From: Lower Merion H.S. (Ardmore, Pennsylvania)	
WT: 212 lbs.	HT: 6 ft. 6 in.	BIRTHDATE: 8/23/78

Kobe Bean Bryant, currently regarded as one of the best players of all times, started playing when he was only three years old. By the time he got to high school, he was an exceptional player and recognized as the top high school player in the country. Instead of attending college, he decided to go directly into the NBA. In the 1996 draft, he was the 13th pick, selected by the Charlotte Hornets. He was traded right away to the Los Angeles Lakers. It is well known that the Lakers told the Hornets to draft him; the Hornets never would have selected Bryant otherwise!

Bryant spent his first three seasons getting used to playing in the NBA, but he got increasingly better each year. By the time Coach Phil Jackson (who helped the Chicago Bulls win six championships) joined the team in 1999, Bryant had become one of the best shooting guards in the league. The Lakers won the National Championship three years in a row (2000-2002)—known as a three-peat—with two basketball stars: Shaquille O'Neal and Kobe Bryant! In later years, Bryant broke many records and became one of the greatest scoring guards in the history of the game. He went on to win two more championships.

WHAT MAKES HIM AN ALL-STAR?

🏀 Bryant is third all-time in NBA history in points scored behind only Kareem Abdul-Jabbar and Karl Malone. He is the L.A. Lakers all-time leading scorer and the fourteenth all-time in steals. He is also the first player in NBA history to have over 30,000 career points and 6,000 career assists.

🏀 Bryant was the MVP of the NBA in 2008; the MVP of the NBA Finals in 2009 and 2010; and the MVP of the All-Star game in 2002, 2007, 2009, and 2011.

🏀 Bryant scored 81-points in a game, which is the second-highest score in NBA history. He also holds the record for making 12 three-point shots in a game.

He has been selected to play in eighteen consecutive All-Star games, the most consecutive All-Star games of any basketball player and one short of the total of any player (a record held by Kareem Abdul-Jabbar)! He also holds the record for most steals all-time in the All-Star games. Kobe announced his retirement in 2016.

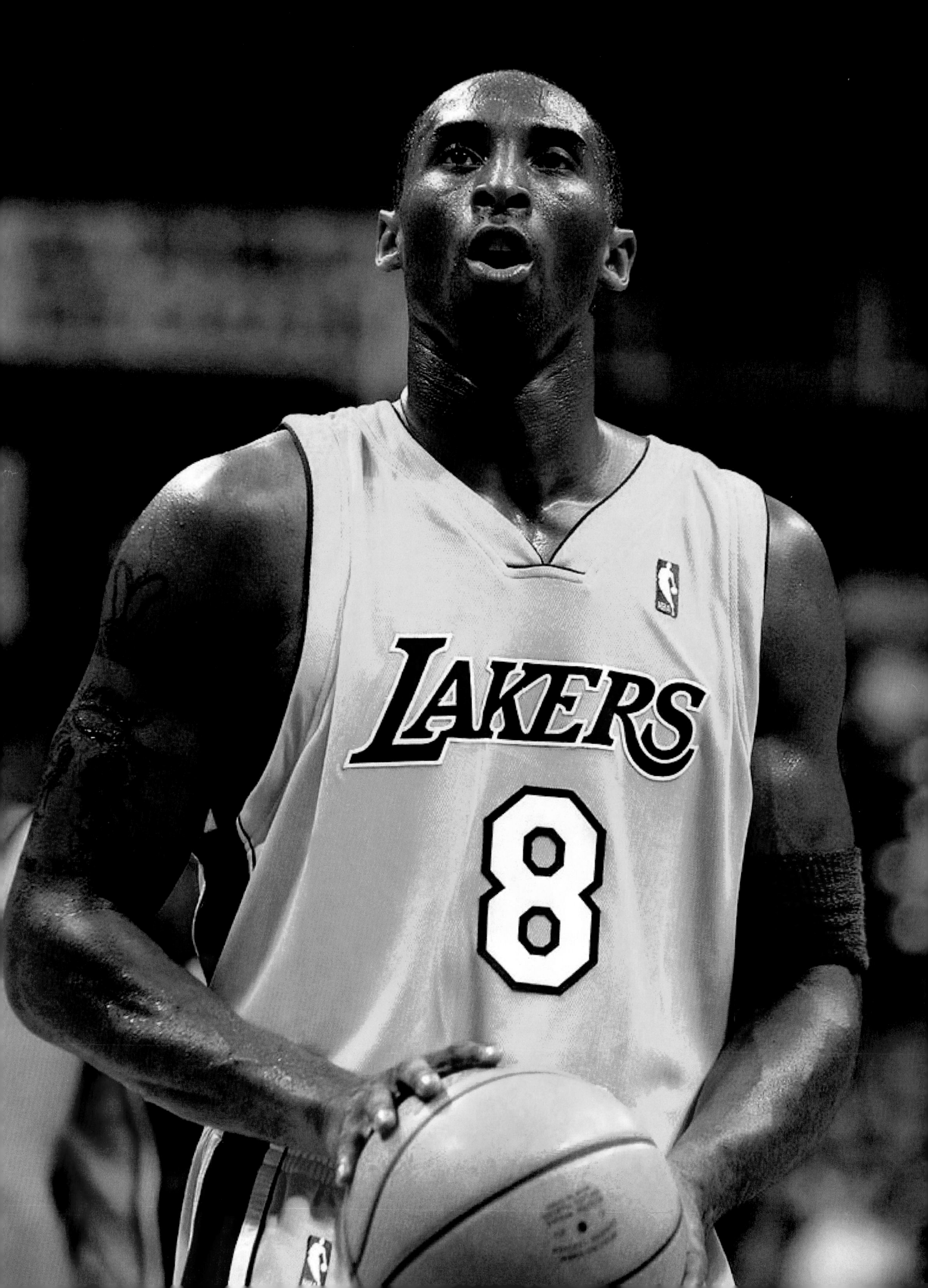
LAKERS
8

THE WEST'S STARTERS

STEPHEN CURRY | WARRIORS

Guard	From: Davidson College (Davidson, North Carolina)	
WT: 190 lbs.	HT: 6 ft. 3 in.	BIRTHDATE: 3/14/88

Wardell Stephen "Steph" Curry II grew up in the basketball life because his father, Dell Curry, was a professional NBA player. Throughout high school, Curry had incredible skills, and he led his team to undefeated seasons, conference titles, and state playoffs.

However, given his size of 6 ft. 0 in. and 160 lbs., he did not receive any scholarship offers from any major basketball schools. Instead, he accepted a scholarship from Davidson, a school that had not won an **NCAA Tournament** since 1969. At Davidson, Curry brought the Davidson Wildcats to the NCAA Tournament twice, and they had their first tournament wins in 2008, beating the Gonzaga Bulldogs, Georgetown Hoyas, and Wisconsin Badgers to make it into the Elite Eight. But then they lost to the Kansas Jayhawks who went on to win the championship. Curry was named the Most Outstanding Player of the Midwest Region for the tournament; he was the first player to win the award from a team not in the Final Four since 1994.

After Steph's junior year, he was picked 7th in the NBA draft by the Golden State Warriors. He came in second in NBA Rookie of the Year voting and won the

WHAT MAKES HIM AN ALL-STAR?

Curry set the NCAA record for the highest number of three-point field goals for a freshman in a single season. His junior year, he set the NCAA three-point record for a single season again, and he was the NCAA's scoring leader.

Curry won the NBA sportsmanship award in 2010, and he was the MVP of the NBA in 2015.

He set a new record for single season three-point field goals in 2013, 2014, and 2015! And he is now on track to set a new record in 2016. Currently, he is #3 all-time in career free-throw percentage. So far, in 2016, he has 10 games with 8 or more three-point shots, which is an NBA record.

NBA All-Star Weekend Skills Challenge. His second year in the NBA, he had injuries and many questioned his strength and size. However, Curry proved everyone wrong and helped the Warriors win the 2015 NBA Championship, becoming the MVP in the process. He has been an All-Star for three years in a row (2014-2016).

KEVIN DURANT | THUNDER

Forward	From: University of Texas (Austin, Texas)	
WT: 240 lbs.	HT: 6 ft. 9 in.	BIRTHDATE: 9/29/88

Kevin "KD the Durantula" Durant played basketball from a young age for several AAU basketball teams and was one of the hottest prospects coming out of high school.

He went to the University of Texas for one season where he became the Naismith College Player of the Year, the first freshman to ever win the award. He left after only one year of college to enter the 2007 NBA Draft and was selected 2nd overall by the Seattle Supersonics.

In his first season, the Supersonics finished 20-62, last in the Western Conference, but KD still won Rookie of the Year—an incredible feat considering his team's record! He was also one of three teenagers to average at least 20 points a game. (King James and Melo were the other two.)

The Supersonics relocated to Oklahoma City and became the Thunder the next year. They also drafted Russell Westbrook. Just one year later (two years after being last in the west), the dynamite duo brought the team to the playoffs, and they have been a constant threat in the Western Conference ever since. KD also won the scoring title three years in a row and became the youngest player to join the 50-40-90 club, which means that he had a shooting percentage of at least 50% for field goals, 40% for three-pointers, and 90% for free throws during one season. He has been an All-Star seven times (2010-2016).

WHAT MAKES HIM AN ALL-STAR?

🏀 KD launched a campaign with KIND snacks called StrongAndKind.com to show that "being kind is not a sign of weakness," and he has contributed money to many good causes, including after-school programs.

🏀 He won all three major rookie of the year awards in college: the AP, Naismith, and John R. Wooden.

🏀 KD won the NBA scoring title four times. He was the MVP of the NBA in 2014. He made the most free throw shots for five years in a row. And he is ranked fourth in the NBA for the highest number of points scored per game over the course of his career.

RUSSELL WESTBROOK | THUNDER

Guard	From: UCLA (Los Angeles, CA)	
WT: 200 lbs.	HT: 6 ft. 3 in.	BIRTHDATE: 11/12/88

Russell Westbrook did not start for his high school team until his junior year, as he was only 5 ft. 8 in. and 140 lbs. Although he had a monster **senior** year, he didn't receive any offers until a player at UCLA decided to go straight to the NBA; Westbrook took the spot! In college, Westbrook was perceived mostly as a defensive player, and he was named as the Pac-10 defensive player of the year. He played for two years at UCLA. Both years, they went to the Final Four of the NCAA Tournament but did not advance further. After that, Westbrook decided to go into the NBA and joined KD with the Thunder.

In his first year with the Thunder, Westbrook proved that he was more than a defensive threat; he was an all-around player who scored a triple-double in March 2009, the first rookie since Chris Paul in the 2005-2006 season and the third in franchise history. In his second year running the offense as the Thunder's full-time point guard, the Thunder went to the playoffs, reversing their last place finish in the Western Conference just two years prior. Westbrook continued to have multiple scoring performances that ranked him among the NBA's best players in history, including recording a triple-double in just twenty minutes, the second fastest in NBA history. He has been an All-Star five times (2011-2013 and 2015-2016).

WHAT MAKES HIM AN ALL-STAR?

🏀 Westbrook played in every game from 2008 through the end of 2013!

🏀 In 2015, he was the NBA scoring champion, and he placed fifth in assists and second in steals.

🏀 Westbrook holds the record for most consecutive games (4 games) with a triple-double (a record he shares with Michael Jordan). He is also tied with Larry Bird for the most points in a game with a triple-double (49 points). And he is one of only three players with more than 40-point triple-doubles in consecutive games.

KAWHI LEONARD | SPURS

Forward	From: San Diego State (San Diego, California)	
WT: 230 lbs.	HT: 6 ft. 7 in.	BIRTHDATE: 6/29/91

Kawhi Leonard grew up in Southern California. When he was a high school senior, he was named Mr. Basketball State Player of the Year. Rather than waiting until the end of his senior year to see what offers he might get, Leonard decided to accept an early offer from San Diego State because of their keen interest in him. He was small for a power forward at the time, but he was an excellent rebounder, and he could even dunk. The San Diego coaches believed not only in his defensive abilities but also in the aggressiveness he would bring to the offensive end.

Leonard was such a hard worker that when he went to college, he brought two lamps from home so that he could set them up in the gym and practice before the school turned on the lights. In college, he was one of four freshmen to lead his team in scoring and rebounding, and he was named the Mountain West Conference Freshman of the Year. After his **sophomore** year, he went into the NBA draft, was selected by the Pacers, and traded immediately to the Spurs.

WHAT MAKES HIM AN ALL-STAR?

⊛ In the 2015 season, he won the Defensive Player of the Year award, the youngest player ever to win the award (a record he shares with Alvin Robertson). He also had the most steals per game.

⊛ Leonard was the third player in NBA history to win both the NBA Defensive Player of the Year award and the NBA Finals MVP award. (The other two players to hold that honor are Michael Jordan and Hakeem Olajuwon.)

⊛ In the 2016 season so far, he leads his team in scoring and has the second highest defensive rating.

The Spurs have made it to the playoffs each year since Leonard joined the team. In his third year, they won the championship and Leonard was the Finals MVP! He was the third youngest player to win the award behind only Magic Johnson, who won it twice before. He was voted to be an All-Star for the first time in 2016.

THE WEST'S RESERVES

LAMARCUS ALDRIDGE	Forward	University of Texas (Austin, TX)		
SPURS	WT: 240 lbs.	HT: 6 ft. 11 in.	BIRTHDATE: 7/19/85	

🏀 After attending two years at the University of Texas, LaMarcus Aldridge was drafted in the first round of the 2006 NBA Draft by the Chicago Bulls. The Bulls draft rights were traded to the Portland Trailblazers, where Aldridge played for nine years, primarily as the star **center** for the team. In 2015, he moved to the Spurs, one of the highest winning teams in league history.

🏀 In the 2014-2015 season, Aldridge made the most field goals (659) of any NBA player. He also made the most two-point field goal attempts of any player in the 2012, 2013, and 2014 seasons. In 2015, he also surpassed Clyde Drexler to take the record for the most rebounds of any Trailblazer. —

🏀 Aldridge has been an All-Star for five years in a row (2012-2016).

DEMARCUS COUSINS	Center/Forward	University of Kentucky (Lexington, Kentucky)		
KINGS	WT: 270 lbs.	HT: 6 ft. 11 in.	BIRTHDATE: 8/13/90	

🏀 DeMarcus Cousins played for one year at University of Kentucky and went to the Elite Eight with teammate John Wall. The Sacramento Kings then selected him in the first round of the NBA draft.

🏀 In April 2015, Cousins became the fourth player in NBA history to have at least 20 points, 20 rebounds, 10 assists, and 5 blocks in a single game. In the very next game, he became the third player in NBA history to have at least 20 points, 20 rebounds, and 10 assists in two consecutive games.

🏀 In the opening game of the 2015-2016 season, Cousins hit 4 out of 5 three-pointers. Up to that point, he had never hit more than 4 three-pointers in an entire season! So far in 2016, he is the only player in the top five for both scoring and rebounding. He was an All-Star in 2015 and 2016.

ANTHONY DAVIS	Center/Forward	University of Kentucky (Lexington, Kentucky)		
PELICANS	WT: 253 lbs.	HT: 6 ft. 10 in.	BIRTHDATE: 3/11/93

🏀 Anthony "The Unibrow" Davis had one of the most dominant college basketball careers in history. As a freshman at Kentucky, he won the Associated Press College Basketball Player of the Year, the John R. Wooden award, the Naismith College of the Year award, the NCAA Tournament Most Outstanding Player award, Defensive Player of the Year award, and more!

🏀 The New Orleans Hornets (later named the Pelicans) picked Davis 1st overall in the 2012 NBA Draft after he played just one year in college. During his second year in the NBA, he became the youngest player to have at least 30 points, 10 rebounds, and 5 blocks in a game. He was also the leader in blocked shots per game for the season.

🏀 Davis was selected to play in three consecutive All-Star games (2014, 2015, and 2016), but he only played in two due to injuries.

DRAYMOND GREEN	Forward	Michigan State University (East Lansing, Michigan)		
WARRIORS	WT: 230 lbs.	HT: 6 ft. 7 in.	BIRTHDATE: 3/4/90

🏀 The Warriors drafted Draymond Green in the second round of the 2012 NBA Draft. Each year, he gained more playing time until he became a starter in 2014 after David Lee was injured. The Warriors played Green in the power forward and center positions, which are very unusual positions for a player of his height. Green uses his strength and speed to help the Warriors play a new breed of "small ball" basketball, a tactic that helped the team win the National Championship in 2015.

🏀 Green has continued his success with 10 triple-doubles in the 2015-2016 season so far, the most triple-doubles made by any Warrior in a season. Green was voted onto his first All-Star team in 2016.

🏀 Not one to forget those who helped him along the way, Green donated $3.1 million dollars to his college, the largest donation made to a college by a basketball player to date.

THE WEST'S RESERVES

JAMES HARDEN	Guard	Arizona State University (Tempe, Arizona)	
ROCKETS	WT: 220 lbs.	HT: 6 ft. 5 in.	BIRTHDATE: 8/26/89

🏀 After playing at Arizona State for two years, James Harden was drafted by the Oklahoma City Thunder with the 3rd overall pick in the 2009 NBA Draft. He was later traded to the Houston Rockets, where his style of shooting three-pointers and driving to the basket fit right in.

🏀 In the 2014-2015 season, Harden had 2 over-50-point games, 10 over-40-point games, and 4 triple-doubles, helping his team clinch the number two seed in the Western Conference. But they lost to the Warriors. That year, Harden was voted MVP for a new award called the National Basketball Players Association (NBPA) Players Award.

🏀 Harden has been named to the All-Star game for four consecutive years (2013-2016).

CHRIS PAUL	Guard	Wake Forest (Winston-Salem, North Carolina)	
CLIPPERS	WT: 175 lbs.	HT: 6 ft. 0 in.	BIRTHDATE: 5/6/85

🏀 Chris Paul grew up working alongside his grandfather in the family's gas station. Heartbroken after his grandfather died at the age of sixty-one, Paul decided he would honor him by scoring 61 points in his high school game the next day. With two minutes left in the game, he drove to the basket, scoring those last two points.

🏀 He attended Wake Forest University and helped his team become the number one team in the country. He left after two years and was selected as the 4th pick overall in the 2005 NBA Draft by the Hornets. In 2011, he was traded to the Los Angeles Clippers.

🏀 Paul won the NBA Rookie of the Year Award, two Olympic gold medals, USA Basketball Male Athlete of the Year, and led the NBA in assists four times and steals six times. He is #11 on the NBA assists list. He has been an All-Star for nine straight years.

| KLAY THOMPSON | Guard | Washington State University (Pullman, Washington) |
| WARRIORS | WT: 215 lbs. | HT: 6 ft. 7 in. | BIRTHDATE: 2/8/90 |

Klay Thompson is the son of former NBA basketball champion Mychal Thompson. Klay is one of four father-son duos to win NBA Championships.

Thompson is known for his pure shooting ability. He and fellow teammate Stephen Curry have been labeled by many as the "best shooting duo" in NBA history. The duo's nickname is "the Splash Brothers." In 2013, they combined to make 483 three-point shots, the most by any duo in NBA history. Then in 2015, they combined to make 525 three-point shots, beating their previous record! In January 2015, Thomson set an NBA record by scoring 37 points in one quarter making all 13 of 13 shots.

Thompson was named an All-Star two years in a row (2015-16). He lost the Three-point Contest in 2015, but he beat Steph Curry in 2016, making them the first teammates to win in back-to-back years.

INJURED PLAYERS

The following players were nominated to play in the All-Star game, but due to injuries, they were replaced before it started. However, they are definitely All-Stars!

CHRIS BOSH | HEAT

Forward	From: Georgia Institute of Technology (Atlanta, Georgia)	
WT: 235 lbs.	HT: 6 ft. 11 in.	BIRTHDATE: 3/24/84

Chris Bosh was drafted by the Raptors in 2003, the same year that LeBron James, Dwyane Wade, and Carmelo Anthony were drafted by their respective teams. That year, he led all rookies in blocks and rebounds. After playing seven years in Toronto, Bosh remains the Raptor's all-time leader in minutes played, rebounds (both offensive and defensive), blocks, free throws attempted (and made), and double-doubles in a single season. He is also Toronto's first player to reach 10,000 points.

After Toronto, Bosh moved on to play with the Miami Heat and was part of two championship teams. Bosh was in nine consecutive All-Star games from 2006-2014 and was again selected in 2016, but he couldn't play due to a calf injury.

Bosh also acts from time to time; he has played roles in the Marvel's Hulk and the Agents of S.M.A.S.H. He also spends a lot of his time raising money for kids in need.

JIMMY BUTLER | BULLS

Guard/Forward	From: Marquette University (Milwaukee, Wisconsin)	
WT: 220 lbs.	HT: 6 ft. 7 in.	BIRTHDATE: 3/25/86

- Jimmy Butler was selected in the first round of the 2011 NBA Draft. By the end of his second season in 2013, he was an important part of the Bulls team, averaging over 40 minutes a game for the team when they went to the playoffs.

- In January 2014, Butler set a record for the Bulls by playing 60 minutes in one game in a triple overtime victory against the Magic.

- He broke another record held by another famous Bulls' player—Michael Jordan—on January 2016 when he scored 40 points in one half! His selection to play in 2016 would have been his second All-Star game, but he couldn't play because of a knee injury.

EXTRA, EXTRA!

SKILLS CONTEST

The All-Star Game Skills Contest, until 2016, had always been reserved for guards and small forwards, those players better known for handling the ball and for their speed. In 2016, the NBA decided to add a wrinkle to the contest and made this contest a dual between the small guys and the big guys (dubbed "the bigs"). The bigs, the centers and power forwards, took on the challenge with a vengeance. Karl-Anthony Towns, selected 1st overall in the 2015 draft by the Minnesota Timberwolves, went up against Isaiah Thomas in the final round. This was truly the perfect example of the small against the big: Thomas is a point guard at 5 ft. 9 in. and Towns is a center at 7 ft. tall! The race was very close, and it came down to a battle of three-point shots at the end of the course. In the end, the bigs took the prize, and all the other big guys showered Towns with hugs and high fives.

SLAM DUNK CONTEST

Many are calling 2016 one of the best Slam Dunk Contests ever! In the end, it came down to a contest between Zach LaVine of the Minnesota Timberwolves, who won the contest in 2015, and Aaron Gordon of the Orlando Magic. The contest went to double-overtime because both players continued to get perfect scores with their outrageous under-the-leg, soaring, spinning, and leaping dunks. Zach LaVine finally won the contest by soaring from the free-throw line with a between-the-legs dunk!

THE RECORD-SETTING 2016 GAME

The 2016 All-Star Game offered viewers quite a few new records for the history books!

 The West scored the most points in a quarter with 52, and the most points in a half with 92.

 The teams scored the most combined points in any game in history with 369!

 Russell Westbrook became the first player to individually win the MVP award in back-to-back years.

 The West's 31 three-point shots and the two teams' 51 combined three-point shots set an All-Star game record.

 Paul George set an individual All-Star game record with 9 three-point shots in the game. With 41 total points, he was only 1 point short of Wilt Chamberlain's record of 42 points! While there hadn't been much defense the rest of the game, it appeared that the West's coach, Gregg Popovich, decided not to let George grab the record too easily. He sent players to double-team George near the end of the game to make it much more difficult for him to get that last point or two.

GLOSSARY

ASSIST – A statistic awarded to a player who passes the ball to a teammate, which results in a made basket.

BACKCOURT – The team's guards, including the point guard and the shooting guard.

DRAFT– A process by which teams take turns selecting players to join their team. The teams have the right to select the players from a group of possible players in a set order. Once the team selects the player, that team has the exclusive right to have that player join that team. In the NBA, the teams each get two selections (unless they have traded their selection to another team). The order of selection is partially based on the teams' records and partially based on a "lottery." The lottery for the top three picks is only for the fourteen teams who did not make the playoffs in the previous season. After those three teams are drawn in the lottery, the remaining teams are ordered based on the reverse order of their winning (or losing record) from the year before.

DRAFTED – When a player is selected in the DRAFT (see above), they have been selected by the team to join that team.

FIELD GOAL – A basket scored from any shot or tap-in (not including free throws). It is worth two or three points depending on how far away the player is from the basket.

FRANCHISE – Sports team.

FRESHMAN – A first-year student at high school or college. See also SOPHOMORE, JUNIOR, and SENIOR.

JUNIOR – A third-year student at high school or college. See also FRESHMAN, SOPHOMORE, and SENIOR.

NCAA TOURNAMENT – The tournament held by the National College Association of America that happens every year in March and leads to "March Madness." The tournament starts with sixty-four teams. It is a single-elimination tournament, which results in a lot of drama! The teams narrow to the SWEET SIXTEEN, ELITE EIGHT, FINAL FOUR, and the final game to win the national championship.

PHILANTHROPIST – A person who freely gives money, time, or services to help out other people or other good causes.

PLAYER POSITIONS – Here are the main basketball player positions.
- GUARD (POINT GUARD / SHOOTING GUARD)
- FORWARD (SMALL FORWARD / POWER FORWARD)
- CENTER

Here is a drawing of the usual positions the players would take in the scoring end of the basketball court. The point guard is often the shortest player on the team; he normally brings the ball down the court and calls out plays for the rest of his teammates. The center is usually the tallest player on the team; he collects the most rebounds and often gets the most blocks.
The other players fall somewhere in between.

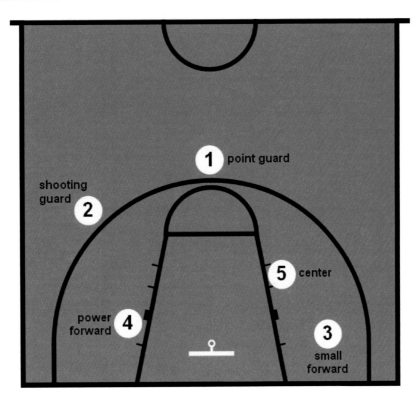

ROOKIE – An athlete in his or her first season on a team.

SENIOR – A student in his or her final year of high school or college, which is usually, but not always, the fourth year of school. See also FRESHMAN, SOPHOMORE, and JUNIOR.

SHOT CLOCK – A timer designed to make the game go faster and make the players score more often. The offensive team must attempt a FIELD GOAL before the shot clock expires.

SOPHOMORE – A second-year student of high school or college. See also FRESHMAN, JUNIOR, and SENIOR.

TRIPLE-DOUBLE – A statistic awarded to a player who achieves a score of 10 or more in three of the following categories in one game: points, rebounds, assists, steals, and blocked shots.

PHOTOGRAPHY CREDITS

Allison, Keith. "Al Horford." Digital image. Wikimedia Commons. November 30, 2013. https://commons.wiki-media.org/w/index.php?curid=29946641

Allison, Keith. "Andre Drummond vs Wizards 2014." Digital image. Wikimedia Commons. January 18, 2014. https://commons.wikimedia.org/w/index.php?curid=30694823

Allison, Keith. "Carmelo Anthony Nov 2013." Digital image. Wikimedia Commons. November 23, 2013. https://commons.wikimedia.org/wiki/File:Carmelo_Anthony_Nov_2013.jpg#/media/File:Carmelo_Anthony_Nov_2013.jpg

Allison, Keith. "Chris Bosh and Hilton Armstrong." Digital image. Wikimedia Commons. December 18, 2010. https://commons.wikimedia.org/wiki/File:Chris_Bosh_and_Hilton_Armstrong.jpg#/media/File:Chris_Bosh_and_Hilton_Armstrong.jpg

Allison, Keith. "John Wall (16614727036)." Digital image. Wikimedia Commons. February 24, 2015. https://commons.wikimedia.org/wiki/File:John_Wall_(16614727036).jpg#/media/File:John_Wall_(16614727036).jpg

Allison, Keith. "John Wall, Stephen Curry (16433225927)." Digital image. Wikimedia Commons. February 24, 2015. https://commons.wikimedia.org/wiki/File:John_Wall,_Stephen_Curry_(16433225927).jpg#/media/File:-John_Wall,_Stephen_Curry_(16433225927).jpg

Allison, Keith. "Kevin Durant Dunk." Digital image. Wikimedia Commons. March 14, 2011. https://commons.wikimedia.org/wiki/File:Kevin_Durant_dunk.jpg#/media/File:Kevin_Durant_dunk.jpg

Allison, Keith. "Kevin Duran Free Throw 2014." Digital image. Wikimedia Commons. June 18, 2014. https://commons.wikimedia.org/wiki/File:Kevin_durant_free_throw_2014.jpg#/media/File:Kevin_durant_free_throw_2014.jpg

Allison, Keith. "Klay Thompson (16614748116)." Digital image. Wikimedia Commons. February 24, 2015. https://commons.wikimedia.org/wiki/File:Klay_Thompson_(16614748116).jpg#/media/File:Klay_Thompson_(16614748116).jpg

Allison, Keith. "Kobe Bryant 2014." Digital image. Wikimedia Commons. December 3, 2014. https://commons.wikimedia.org/wiki/File:Kobe_Bryant_2014.jpg#/media/File:Kobe_Bryant_2014.jpg

Allison, Keith. "Kyle Lowry (17283761882)." Digital image. Wikimedia Commons. April 26, 2015. https://commons.wikimedia.org/wiki/File:Kyle_Lowry_(17283761882).jpg#/media/File:Kyle_Lowry_(17283761882).jpg

Allison, Keith. "LaMarcus Aldridge1." Digital image. Wikimedia Commons. December 3, 2008. https://commons.wikimedia.org/w/index.php?curid=6322260

Allison, Keith. "LeBron James (15662939969)." Digital image. Wikimedia Commons. November 21, 2014. https://commons.wikimedia.org/wiki/File:LeBron_James_(15662939969).jpg#/media/File:LeBron_James_(15662939969).jpg

Allison, Keith. "Paul Millsap Atlanta Hawks cropped." Digital image. Wikimedia Commons. November 30, 2013. https://commons.wikimedia.org/w/index.php?curid=34902988

Allison, Keith. "Stephen Curry Shooting." Digital image. Wikimedia Commons. March 2, 2011. https://commons.wikimedia.org/wiki/File:Stephen_Curry_shooting.jpg#/media/File:Stephen_Curry_shooting.jpg

Allison, Keith. "Stephen Curry vs Washington 2016." Digital image. Wikimedia Commons. February 3, 2016. https://commons.wikimedia.org/w/index.php?curid=46777124

"Basketball Positions." Digital image. Wikimedia Commons. May 17, 2007. https://commons.wikimedia.org/w/index.php?curid=2119628

Basket Streaming Photography. "Zach Lavine." Digital image. Flickr. February 13, 2016. https://www.flickr.com/photos/basketstreaming/24630547409/in/photolist-DZeX2e-DwvZCv-DYR7Pc-DWEkuC-E5Loaw-CLis3E-DaGzwc-DEYDGs-CRpWEd

Bazemore, Kent. "Draymond Green at Warriors Open Practice." Digital image. Wikimedia Commons. October 13, 2012. https://commons.wikimedia.org/w/index.php?curid=23516578

Chen, Derral. "James Harden Rockets cropped." Digital image. Wikimedia Commons. December 21, 2012. https://commons.wikimedia.org/w/index.php?curid=23283992

Chensiyuan. "Demar derozan 2009." Digital image. Wikimedia Commons. Accessed February 6, 2010. https://commons.wikimedia.org/wiki/File:Demar_derozan_2009.jpg#/media/File:Demar_derozan_2009.jpg

Drost, Erik. "Dwyane Wade 20151030." Digital image. Wikimedia Commons. October 30, 2015. https://commons.wikimedia.org/w/index.php?curid=44669276

Drost, Erik. "Russell Westbrook dribbling vs Cavs (cropped)." Digital image. Wikimedia Commons. January 25, 2015. https://commons.wikimedia.org/wiki/File:Russell_Westbrook_dribbling_vs_Cavs_(cropped).jpg#/media/File:Russell_Westbrook_dribbling_vs_Cavs_(cropped).jpg

Gaertner, Jacob. "Jimmy Butler." Digital image. Wikimedia Commons. May 8, 2015. https://commons.wikimedia.org/w/index.php?curid=46034504

joshuak8. "Paul George Pacers." Digital image. Wikimedia Commons. March 5, 2014. https://commons.wikimedia.org/w/index.php?curid=31545591

Larrison, Jim. "Paul Gasol high five with Stryde at the end of the Chicago Bulls game." Digital image. Wikimedia Commons. January 17, 2015. https://commons.wikimedia.org/w/index.php?curid=38086176

Lee, Joseph A. "Kobe Bryant 8." Digital image. Wikimedia Commons. October 12, 2009. https://commons.wikimedia.org/wiki/File:Kobe_Bryant_8.jpg#/media/File:Kobe_Bryant_8.jpg

Lew, Stephen. "Kawhi Leonard." Digital image. Icon Sportswire Photography and Corbis Images.

Mike. "Demarcus Cousins Dec 2013." Digital image. Wikimedia Commons. December 21, 2013. https://commons.wikimedia.org/w/index.php?curid=30410801

Mike. "Isaiah Thomas Dec 2013." Digital image. Wikimedia Commons. December 21, 2013. https://commons.wikimedia.org/w/index.php?curid=30421910

Montanari, Luca. "Three Point Contest." Digital image. Diggita.it. February 14, 2016. http://www.diggita.it/v.php?id=1519395

Tony the Tiger. "Anthony Davis Dunk." Digital image. Wikimedia Commons. January 1, 2014. https://commons.wikimedia.org/wiki/File:20140101_Anthony_Davis_dunk_(1).JPG#/media/File:20140101_Anthony_Davis_dunk_(1).JPG

Verse Photography. "Chris Paul floater 20131118 Clippers v Grizzles." Digital image. Wikimedia Commons. November 18, 2013. https://commons.wikimedia.org/wiki/File:Chris_Paul_floater_20131118_Clippers_v_Grizzles.jpg#/media/File:Chris_Paul_floater_20131118_Clippers_v_Grizzles.jpg

Made in the USA
Middletown, DE
05 April 2018